# She Will Rise

# She Will Rise

Kara Troglin

She Will Rise
© 2018 Kara Troglin

Kara Troglin
karatroglin@gmail.com

ISBN 978-0-578-42346-3

Printed in the United States of America
First Printing, 2018

Editing: Tell Tell Editing | telltellpoetry.com
Design: Heather McIntyre, Cover&Layout |
www.coverandlayout.com
Cover Photo by Farsai Chaikulngamdee on Unsplash

For my grandma, Betty Morgan,
and my mother, Nancy Troglin

# She Will Rise

# Trigger Warning

Domestic abuse
Emotional abuse
Relationships
Self-harm
Sexual assault
Suicidal ideation


Please seek self-care while reading topics throughout this book to avoid being triggered.

# Acknowledgements

I would like to express my deepest gratitude to my amazing and strong-willed mother. She has been with me every single step of the way, the tears, laughter, pain, and joy. She encouraged me to follow my dreams, even when that meant leaving far from home to the other side of the world. I can't thank her enough for being there any time of day or night and most importantly showing me how to never, ever give up.

My grandmother, for her unconditional love, continuous support, and being my best friend since I was a little girl. Thank you for all that you have done for me.

Kallie Falandays, my editor at Tell Tell Poetry, for giving me honest feedback and efficiently working to help me turn this book into a reality. I'm truly thankful for all your hard work.

My teachers of Zuna Yoga, for giving me an amazing YTT experience in Bali and providing me with the knowledge of yoga and meditation that has changed my life in the most healing way.

My muse and main source of inspiration for this book. I will always, always love you.

Lastly, I want to thank all my family, friends, and teachers near and far, currently present or long removed, who inspired me in this path of life. You have each brought something incredibly beautiful into my world and I am forever grateful. This book wouldn't be possible without any of you.

# Contents

*Do one thing every day
that scares you.*

—Eleanor Roosevelt

# 1

# She'll Sleep
# for Winter

# A Woman Who Writes

Dear love, I am that woman
Who feels too much.
No matter how morose or cold or tired
I still rise like the sun in this dark place
Spinning stars and flowers in my hair
A strange goddess who will soon
Reconcile again with the moon.

# These Days

The boreal forest sleeps undisturbed in snow,
the animals have crawled into their spaces,
closing down their eyes for winter.
A moose slumbers outside my bedroom,
his antlers curled, his gaze steady, noiseless.

All I ever do now is stare out my window,
watch the sun begin to wane.
A stellar jay soars swoops of air
with his wild wings,
in the silver clouds—*skreeka! skreeka!*

Loneliness wakes in my bones,
the forest grows darker, and I think
how I slip in and out of my own life.

# October

I can hear the early morning birds croon,
warble and trill in the distance.
They are telling me something important.

It is a frigid, autumn temper,
bone-chilling and empty,
as I hold myself in a fetal position

beneath the feathered duvet,
my cold hands on my stomach.
I grow sharp with a gulp.

Heaviness comes over my eyes
as I barely bring myself to mutter
a finalized goodbye.

# Some Winters Are Harder than Others

In some strange way, the birds of my neighborhood
climb the thick sky-circle, a wayside blue that drowns
my ice-age dreams; mountains of solid darkness
tower overhead with the triumph of glaciers
waking in winter, starless and destructive.

This ghost town sleeps covered in snow
and I take from our house the darker thoughts
into the moon-blued waves of the earth.
Listening to the bells of the Pacific
and the aftermath of burnt-out calamity, ice-ribbed
boats sink where human hands have failed.

Overnight, an albatross of white frost
crosses the lake we once dipped our ankles in.

# This Is What It Feels Like

If I only live one life then I want to soak
All the beauty into my veins and breathe
The wild air deep into my lungs and blossom.

We are an evolving humanity who can choose
To love or hate. I want nothing more than to
Become the joy women dream about.

# Drowning

Beautiful things come from the dark.

At times I meditate for the heartache to end.

I fear one day it will swallow me whole.

# She'll Sleep for Winter

The hoarfrost on tips of trees
retracts color and pierces
back into my eyes,
into the soft, sleepy dream
from which I am desperately trying
to wake.

Will I ever shake the sullen slumber
that fell from the landscape
into my existence?

Suddenly, the snow begins
and all around is
white
white
white
mountain peaks.
I think of you, but
it is too cold to move.

# Somewhere in Alaska

A man sleeps at the base of a mountain;
when he wakes, he carries a guitar
into the streets of the town where he lives
and sings to wayward travelers
with silver in his voice,
and silky sounds of home.

He often thinks of his family, the stubbornness
that led him to find this town's dark winters,
wind roaring across the gulf, shaking windows
and doors. His old blue house reflects
the bay waters he looks at every day,
sometimes without noticing that even
the dull electric blue consumes gloom.

# Sleeping in My Skin

In the morning I am splitting cells
in half, bringing down the knife
on a perfectly green apple, circling
the inward spine, seeds spilling over
onto the wood counter space.

If I could pull apart the pieces
and drown them with ice water or tea
leaves, maybe I would feel better
about having to say goodbye
to the drowsed woman
lingering behind my eyes.

# Still Someone

It has been years
since I last saw you,
but who is counting
the months
or seasons
on a clock, or the miles
from my state to yours

because haven't we all
had someone on our
mind when we wake up
for the first second out of sleep,
the vulnerable, groggy-eyed,
heart beats
"if only."

# Snow Moon

I see you hiding behind the clouds to the left
of the white-capped mountain peaks;
across the bay, you are rising like a woman.

Mysterious moon listening to breath,
watching deep sleep, curled into bed.
Will you keep your white light shining above me always?

Will you share with me the conundrum of life?
Will you show me who to love?
For all the times I have lost,

I know you will rise burning again
even when my drowsy eyes close
and I'm heavy with too much gravity.

Please,
fall into me.

# Savvy Traveler

I do not know how you came into this space,
maybe when I was sleeping or felt a song curl

my loneliness minutes from letting go.
But you found me and somehow opened

the hinged door to the inside
that I so fiercely kept from showing.

(It seems you picked the lock with your gentle words.)
I do not know what it is about you

that keeps me coming back,
but in this space I will continue to welcome

your soft touch, hands that subtract the weight
of my tears, my heavy heart lies with yours,

and I feel the most important part of love:
acceptance.

When you leave this city,
you will be taking a small part of me

that is reserved for you. And I will sit
by the wayside and wonder about you,

remembering the way
we fell in love,

if even for only one hour.

# Sleeping Lady

We were driving down the highway
along an open road I take every day,
but this time I intently observed
the mountainous shapes and colors.

Denali peering in the background
with sharp, rigid peaks.
Sapphire sky
and crisp, cloudless air.

Then there she was hiding
in the landscape, the body
of a woman, the way her breast
rounded softly as she lies on her back,

chin up, asleep deep in rosy snow,
alpine glow.
I wanted to become her,
surrendered to the earth.

# My Love, Why Have You Left Me Alone?

I wish to tell you how often I think of you.
Sometimes it is with tenderness when I am
reminded of your touch and how our two bodies
slept nestled beneath flannel sheets, strong hands
reaching to find my soft body before the sun rises.

I long to be held close to you again
as you enter my thoughts, even during
dish washing or as
I trek these coniferous peaks.
It is you that hits my chest as I inhale
for breath and look out across the high seas.

When I am driving in my car the frosted
snow falls onto the windshield and my face
swells hot with tears at the thought of how long
it has been since we last touched one another.

I want to be the woman you love.
It seems simple, but I find myself
wondering why you are so far from me.

The distance invites longing into our world
and I have tried to love another, but it is you
who has left this trace on my soul.
I must get back to you, no matter the waves.

# I Let Him Go

It is not love
that causes pain,
it is not love that is difficult,
nor the sadness that visits me often,
but it is the way the world turns itself
in the universe and how we
drift between.

It is fear that pulls you away from me,
and to think I am not good enough
for you is a foolish lie.
Ha! I am a woman beyond
your hands,
you try to grasp
as I slip away,
but I have already left you.

I let him go.
I let him go.
She is gone.

# The Hurt

I traced my fingers along the stars of your spine
as the full flower moon grew big in the sky.
I wanted to keep your image like this
for the rest of my life
because I knew it wasn't going to last.

I knew you were going to fall asleep soon
and in two months we would be sleeping
in separate beds, in separate houses
in search of someone else,
trying to erase the memory
of our warm bodies next to one another.

# When Other Times Arrive

It's winter now as I walk past
the old rock where we sat together.
I reminisce on summer days
wearing the OM skirt you bought me
while eating a succulent peach
I bought from the health food store,
teeth sinking into the silk skin.

We were happy that day
and you took my picture in the sunshine,
the silhouette of my willowy body
outlined in rays of light,
my long hair shining flaxen
against the blue ocean water.

You looked up at me with luminous eyes
as though you were deciding to keep me
by your side forever. All the years
and at last we were in the same place again.

It is now seasons later as I stare
at this dulled rock, gathering snow
and frozen ice on its seat.
The dark ocean is nearly black, roaring
with winter waves, white caps, deep swells.
Some things are just not meant to be forever.

# Forgiveness

I am alone in a pitch-black room in Alaska
thinking about the meaning of happiness
and how to obtain its feathery features.
To feel a smile teeming with unreflecting
love and a magic hand that keeps the
divine light lit.

Quietly, I seek meaning.

I am reminded of the malevolent
words that left imprints of insecurity
and the misuse of hands on my body
that quieted my spirit, the very essence
of who I am taken with indifference.

I learn to let go and forgive
the history of you and me,
the memories of a haunted past,
and begin, one by one,
to open myself up again
like the petals of a white lotus flower.

# Silence

Tonight I laid in the bathtub
and thought about what it would be like
to die.

I breathed in deep eucalyptus oil
and immersed my body into
hot water.

I watched my chest rise
and fall with each passing breath
as salty tears welled.

The burnt candlelight flickering
in the corner of the room
as steam rose in humid air.

I let myself float in this silent space
until it was time to unplug
the drain.

No one would ever understand
why she ended her life
or what they could have done better.

Maybe her pain was so unbearable
and she wanted to finally
get some sleep.

# My Love Life

I don't really know if any man
I've been with has loved me.
I have heard the words spoken, sung, serenaded
into my ears, been lifted up and spun around
a dance floor, even softly spread
across my bed with legs open
while the man caresses my body,
whispering, "You are beautiful."

But I have never had a man
grab my face with his hands
when I am shaking,
weeping, as he looks deep
into my blue eyes to whisper,
"You are safe with me."

I have been a giver to men
who have taken, cursed, stolen,
shoved me into a shattered mirror
then left me curled into a bed of tears.
Alone.

I learn to fall in love with myself.
Goddess, radiating light, eloquent dancer,
spinning my dress on a summer's eve.
I will always be there for me.

# The Second Time You Said Goodbye

The loneliest air outside is bitter;
when I breathe I can feel my lungs freeze,
voice stuck in my throat, eyelashes catching
snowflakes, a sinking solitude.
Moon jellys lie frozen on the beach,
snow geese in flight, my heart is broken.
Icy sharpness, somnolent mornings,
someone tell me the truth about love.

Is it the daunting winter season
looming above our heads
that ended our sweet embrace?
Is it the darkness, the deep cold water,
that led you away from me,
keeps me hiding in my warm sanctuary?
I have never felt so afraid to say goodbye,
and these piles of snow are taller than my body.

I shovel and bend and shove and scream
until I can no longer move.
I think of you, my small frame fatigued.
Always tired, you know I am always tired,
from taking everything in
with my eyes, my hands, my touch,
my sensitivity and observation, my love
overwhelms and leaves me weary-eyed.

# Questions

These scars on my heart
are telling me not to love you.
You don't lean in to give me
a hug or a kiss on the cheek goodbye
because you think the girl
at the end of your bar is pretty,
and you're "just doing your job."

But then tell me, why is it
when you watch a man watch my hips sway
you can't help yourself to my body?
Claiming me as your own.
You don't get to have me
when it's convenient for you.

You'll only find yourself
alone at night in your bed
without me,
writing songs about other women,
but wishing they were me.

# Women

When a woman lies her body down next to a man
she is telling him, "Here is the deepest part of me,
the secret space." She will wrap her vivacious legs
around him, push the body forward, and breathe.
It is within this innocent moment all is abandoned.
Do not destroy her. She is offering herself.

The female body is more than her physical frame.
She is more than irresistible, sensual energy
with rounded breasts, thighs that know
how to press against another body.
Do you know who she is?
Do you know what makes up the sacred space?

If you cannot offer her honesty in the purest form
or connect to the beautiful woman on the inside,
then you do not deserve her perfect body.
For a woman is powerful yet vulnerable;
do not take from her what does not belong to you.

# Rise

In the frost of the winter's morning
I walk along the water's edge
after a blue moon tide.
The frigid air runs down my spine
as I inhale the ocean's song,
listening to the tug and pull
of water lapping on rocks.

It is the dawning of day,
slant golden light, fresh and new,
nestled sea creatures rise to sing.
This early morning walk grants me
a second waking to a vast universe.
What is the life I should live?

# Speak

Be very, very careful with your words.
They can cause more damage
than you will ever know.

If I wore the pain on my face
he caused in my heart
I would be covered in bruises.

# January

It was a moonless night, endless sky,
the night you left me
standing alone in my black coat.

It was the coldest of the year
as I begged you do not go.
The sadness consuming me.

# Waiting for You

I want to be in the arms
of a man who knows
he wants to sleep next to me
and wrap his legs with mine.

I can hear the shrilling break
when you look at me with love
in your eyes, but you also say
"I cannot be the man
to promise you forever."

You don't love me
like you
used to.

# Under a Cold Moon

The moon is full and perfect above our town
and I leave you sleeping snug in bed
as I tiptoe to the still water's edge.

I am standing alone under a cold moon
and feel free deep in my bones
as I look across the ethereal sea with open hands.

I have never been in such a quiet place before,
where mother earth speaks in whispers to you.
She is guiding me into pure abandonment.

# My Black Shroud

How do I tell you it hurts
every morning I wake up?
I lie in the shadows of my past.
The ghosts of lies and deception
follow me into sleep.
We drift together.
We float in and out
of terrible memories.

How do I lie next to you without
waking you with my weeping?
I want to trust you.
I want to believe you are not someone
who will break me.
I want to believe something beautiful
exists for us.
I want to love you without the fear
of you leaving me.

What did I do to deserve this
foreboding fear?
Behind my eyes are tears,
behind my heart is love.
I can't imagine why you would want
to sleep next to me when my skin crawls
with haunted memories
I am desperately trying to forget.

# Somnolent Night

Silver, drowsy rain
falls around me;
blue pine-chills, wet-hooded
hair, heavy black coat
to hide my sullen frame.

Nostalgia fills my cup
of lavender tea
as I sit on the front porch
contemplating the meaning of life
beneath exhausted stars.

I write words in my head
and listen to elemental drops
soak into the soil. Pitter-patter
on the rooftop. I am unconventionally
morose. When will I sleep?

# Pretend Wife

My mother always told me
to find a man who will
be exactly what you need him to be.

And to think,
he almost had me fooled
into believing I was The One

when he had
no intention of keeping me.

# The Night I Knew We Ended

I waited patiently for him tonight,
eager to hold his hands, rub his feet
with my feet, share my adoration.

He tiptoed quietly into bed,
pulled the covers over us;
finally my love had arrived.

But something strange happened.
As he climbed into bed next to me
there was no acknowledgement.

No "I love you" or "I missed you."
Instead came suffocating in my throat
that our time together was over.

How painful it is to lie there and wait
for you when suddenly I realize
you are many moons away from me.

I can still hear your words "I don't fucking care."
Followed with feelings of loneliness.
What am I even doing here?

# Rouge

I am beginning to realize
you were never the man
I thought you were.

I never fell in love with
who you really are
because you kept yourself hidden so well.

It wasn't until you revealed
the face beneath the mask
that I started to see your cold eyes.

I do not miss who you are.
I miss the man you pretended to be.

# After He Left

There was a time I almost gave up
on this beautiful life.
It was a moonless night
and feelings of worthlessness

consumed my mind.
I sought poetry, melatonin,
meditation, any type of peace
I could get my shaking hands on.

His words echoed
inside my body, and the pain
became unbearable.
How could a man who claims

to want to spend the rest of his life
with me suddenly disappear?
Perhaps I am too much woman to love?
I stayed in my bed swallowing grief,

denial, and loss of the life I worked
so hard to create, suddenly taken
away for his egotistical endeavor
to be a lowly bachelor musician.

Oh darling,
who will listen to my story?

How does one learn to trust again?
Gasping for breath between tears,
I contemplated how close I was
to the tipping point, to the end.

# Twist of Fate

I never told anyone who you were
behind closed doors because you
threatened me with your words.

If anyone knew what I knew,
if everyone heard what you said,
you would be left alone.

My mother says karma
is coming for you.
I hope she is right.

# Listen

You don't get to have me
When it's convenient for you.

Please stop coming back
When you get lonely.

I am more woman than you
Ever acknowledged.

# Ganesha

The doctors say my illness
is debilitating. Sometimes
it means it is afternoon when
I finally rise out of bed.
I take a long, hot shower
that turns into a bath
and I lie there trying
to wake up. It is hours
before my day begins.
My eyes water, I have
hollow bags beneath
my baby blues and I feel
like I am floating in air.
This is what depression
feels like. Sometimes
I finally get dressed, put on
my favorite purple sweater
covered in flowers so no one
will see the weight of my eyes.
I can barely keep them open
and I think of him not living
his life with mine.
I miss our tiny dog.
I miss when he would
stare at me as though
he were contemplating
how to ask me to be his wife.
I am heartbreak. I am debilitated.
I am in and out of a hospital bed
because I cannot function in this life
like I used to. Physically my body
is healthy, but my brain is crying.

They say I am on life support.
I ponder death every day as a
way to escape into peaceful slumber.
Why isn't the world more soft?
Why are we always in a rush to get
to the next place without regard
for other people? The humans with
beating hearts and organs who are
trying to survive. My sensitivity
is my superpower. I don't want to
hurt anyone, I just want to rest
and stop feeling sharp, emotional
pain like a dagger down my wrists.
I beg of you please be careful with
the world. I chant to Ganesha,
remover of obstacles,
Om Gam Ganapataye Namah
Om Gam Ganapataye Namah
Om Gam Ganapataye Namah
Remove this pain, this depression,
this darkness hovering above earth.
Replace it with light and peace,
purify our body, mind, spirit, soul.

# Room with a View

In the hospital from the fourth floor
I've been staring outside my large window
across the bitter black treetops
to the misty mountain
lying on her back, Sleeping Lady.

I hear my brain reverberate
"You must not only stay alive
for other people,
but you must continue to
stay alive for yourself."

        When the nurse asks me what prevents me
           from following through with intent:
              The people I love.

# Bones

When the first sign of termination dust
falls onto the orange mountain peaks
the people begin to burrow
themselves into their heavy coats
as the wind blows her secrets
across the deep ocean salt.

The sun is beginning to sleep
and I think I will join her.
In my bedroom, ivy flowers
grow up the tiny bones of my spine
like a spider as the white moon
beckons the call of wintertide.

I am three continents of gardens
and my shade of earthly green
is greeting ghostly figures.
Now I begin to close my eyes and
curl into the warm bed of my vertebrae.
This is the way winter speaks.

# My Wish

For all the hurting souls, I hear you. I know you are there. I hope one day humanity chooses to change the way she rules and positions herself amongst us. My wish is for everyone to be a little more soft and aware of the space they take up, more vulnerable and sensitive.

As of late, there has been little release in my life. The common theme is survive, survive, survive this next hour, day, week, month, year. The seasons are waning in my favor, yet I am groggy-eyed riding the moon-blued waves. I am very, very tired.

Ask yourself, where can I be a little more soft? A little more sensitive to this beating heart inside of me, this beating heart standing right in front of me? Why do some disbelieve, ridicule, taunt others when our world is hurting enough already? Let us be broken, yet mended by the strength it takes to speak up and listen. We are in this spinning universe together.

I love you all.

*You gain strength, courage
and confidence by every
experience in which you really
stop to look fear in the face.
You are able to say to yourself,
'I have lived through this
horror. I can take the next
thing that comes along.'
You must do the thing you
think you cannot do.*

—Eleanor Roosevelt

# 2

# She'll Wake
# for Solstice

# Letting Things Slip

I love not knowing what the day will bring,
when I wake to the sound of wanton rain
against my window and the dogwood
tree blooming white as tulips rise.

I love when I meet someone
and I will write them postcards or send
corsage orchids to plant in the kitchen
(even when the heart is open and breaking).

I love the yellow house down the road
and all the cats that live there with a garden
in the front yard, the granular soil, daffodils,
blue shutters that hide the love I once created
and then tore apart.

# Fig Tree

I could never decide what to do.
You're not the only one
who wakes up
to a changed mind.

One day we loved each other
and we were going to move
to Japan or Indonesia,
drink hot tea by the sea,

or build a treehouse
and plant tulip bulbs
in large yellow tubs
so I could feel happiness

when I didn't believe in it.

None of that happened.

Like the branches of a fig tree
we grew into separate lives,
each one with fat purple fruit
beckoning something else.

# Good-Hearted Man

When I say I love you,
it means my heart is shaking
for the all the days
I want to spend with you.

When I say I love you,
I mean it.
Especially when I am far away,
know even then,
you are the light
I want to share with mine.

# Luminous Lady of the Moon

Her skin is as white as snow
like a rare pearl in his hand.
He watched her take shape,
a beautiful woman all the men
want to drink like blue air.

She is soft, lustrous, stimulating
as she walks into the room
and turns the gloomy, sombre
mood into a radiant and pure light.

# Inspired

It all began to make sense.
The love she had for these men,
each one offering something unique,
to add to her story, her tapestry of life,
singing her song from her mountaintop;
she wasn't sad to say goodbye.

Now there is elation,
acceptance, weaving
each one into her artwork.
For she will always remember
those who stopped by,
how they said her name,
how they struck fire in her eyes.

You may have taken from me,
but I have made you my muse.

# I Knew Him Once

I would have said yes
if he asked me to marry him.
I would have been the woman
to lift the weight off his back,
to give him soft, but fierce love,
to sweetly touch his chin.
I would have loved him every morning
as we washed the sleep from our eyes,
small movements, gentle caresses, warm espresso.

I would have kissed him in every creative way,
mindfully wrapping my body around his,
serenading his skin, leaving prints behind.
I would have loved him as he grew old,
showed him that age was only more reason
to never let go, graying hair, changing face.
I would have loved him always,
if only he would let me.

# Bliss

The men in my family don't know how to talk to me.
There is a type of hostility which emerges beneath
the surface and boils over into a giant flame.
I know they desperately want to save me
from the darkness I have migrated towards.

However, if they knew the blissful soul
I have cultivated over the years they would
witness me swimming in bright light.
If I could tell them one thing,
please believe I am right where I want to be.

# Life Force

The most important thing you have
is your breath.

Do not underestimate the power
that already exists within you.

Right now you are holding
the entire universe

between the confines
of your own heart

and if you are still enough
you can transcend into this healing space.

# April

In the kitchen I'm wearing
a blue dress with polka dots,
slicing a peach with the window open.
I smell the cut grass filtering through,
the cat's meow chasing the squirrel,
and in this moment is all the stillness
I'll ever need. Your hand on my waist,
a slip of sunshine in my yellow hair,
humming a tune to satisfy the heart.
The sudden and unexpected feeling
of joy. Here we are dancing
on our mountaintop.

# Tonsina Point

When I miss him and the life he promised
to build with me I feel the pain of healing.

I am nostalgic for the perfect days
lying on an Alaskan beach
warm in sunshine
ocean waves quietly
lapping the silted shore
with saltwater tears,
glacial sand between toes,
love deep in my heart,
and our tiny dog asleep on my chest,
thinking I had found the life
I wanted to always live
until I wake up and it is gone.

# Queens Park, New Westminster

It is the last days of March
and the city is sprouting dogwoods
while the forest air smells like spring.
I wait for you in the afternoon.
I wait for you in your new city,
observing where you will find
a place to call home.
It is quiet here; the cars,
voices, birds blend together peacefully.
I know you will be happy
and I hope to return to you.
When I do, maybe I will be healthy again,
maybe we can love each other
without having to say goodbye.

# The Waves We Give

Sometimes healing does not
feel good.

Sometimes it means facing
your darkness with waves
of ocean water or keeping
the curtains closed at
two in the afternoon
while other times
you are pure sunshine
in the middle of a boreal forest
hearing birds sing your song
or dancing barefoot with
a stranger on a foreign beach.

Whatever the healing looks like
in this moment watch
how it flows into your space.
Trust the process.
You are fluid,
turbulent particles.

# I Have Not Forgotten

You will be with me always,
even after you have left.
For you have looked deeply
into my eyes and whispered
your story onto my heart.

Our love was written
before we ever met.
This is how we knew
there was something
to hold when our bodies
finally touched.

# Somewhere in Texas

When I wake in the morning I will walk across the field
into the dried mud and black-billed magpies
sleeping in twigs to the place where death has been before,
to the place where there is pain for a daughter,
or a mother, half asleep from summer and five o'clock martinis.

When I get there I will wave my hands at the sky
and think of my father in the August heat, and his father,
or the one before him like an old stone tree.
I cannot cage the minutes or help but wonder
who will forgive me for the things I do?

# Vagabond

I've always had a taste
for traveling alone.
Feet on the ground, head in the sky,
I've got plenty of time
to explore. I've never seen
so much light
when I'm running around
the world with messy hair
surrounded with deep seas,
strange stories, adventurous
moments turned into shades
of forever memories.

No one else
but my true self.

# All I Ever Wanted

I've searched
for someone somewhere
to call home.

I cannot help who I love
and it's always been you.

Let's grow old together
as the sun breaks a glimmer blue;
let me be someone
warm beside you.

# Wake Up

She will rise in the morning
with morose eyes and a heart
full of broken shards.

The night was full of memories
and haunted nightmares of ghosts
from her past who fooled her.

Nonetheless, she will rise
like the sun in this dark place
and share her story with peace.

It is the quiet stillness
that keeps her existing
even when she is hurt.

She is here.

She is brave.

She is rising.

# Healing

Do not judge what you
do not know. If I can
share my story with at least
one person on this earth who
chooses to survive their hurt
then I have done what I needed
to do as a woman, teacher, writer.

# Dharma

Do you ever wonder
if birds question
the meaning of life?
Or maybe they
are so engrossed
with circling the sky?
Focused on survival
and migrating to warmth.

I want to wake up
and sing my song
even if my eyes
are crying.

We are all survivors
on this earth.
We are all migrating
seasons with our
souls craving bliss.

Follow your passion
and never stop believing
in your unique gift
even when you question
your worth. You exist
for a reason.

# I Am Love, I Am Light

Sometimes I worry I am too much
or not enough. Maybe if I was more sociable
or lovely, maybe if I wasn't so irritable
or anxious, would you love me more?

I do not want to change who I am.
It has taken me twenty-eight years
to love this woman.
All the dreams and values
harvested to better my wellness.

I want to live as healthy and as happy
as I can. I want to wake in the morning
and meditate. I want to spend time
with my soul and breathe all of the earth
into my body. I want to flow with the ocean
and sway with the bird's song.

My hips carry the strength of courage,
my lips whisper the secret of love.
I will give it to anyone who wants it.
Deeply manifesting this strange world
into the one of which I have always dreamed.

I have known anxiety since I was
a young girl and now as I grow into this
womanly shape I still possess days
where it takes everything in me to get out
of my bed, to walk out the front door,
to show up in the world,
often despite tears in my eyes.
I am still smiling because I believe in love.

No matter how many times my heart is broken,
no matter how many people
ignore my story, I am alive today.
I believe in light. The source that brings
all living things to move and thrive.

I believe I am here to love a world
that needs deep healing.

So please do not take this away from me.
If I am not enough for you, if I make you angry,
then let me go so I can be who I need to be
in this marvelous world.

Let me live amongst the tall trees, let me saturate myself
in color and return to where I came from, let me love
the green plants, let me love the blueblack ocean's tide,
let me breathe everything I am made of into my body
so that I can keep loving this shaking spirit.

I am the peaceful poetry of Mother Earth.

# The Phoenix

You can't change
what has happened to you.

But you can love
yourself through it.

This is how you
rise from the ashes.

Burn your fire,
take flight with wings,

never stop believing
in your magic, baby.

# Gift

My depression showed me
the most powerful thing
I will ever know.

You are never alone.

Take this darkness
and turn it into
your healing power

to connect with all
living beings
on this sacred earth.

# Heart Sutra

Darling, you must be tired
of searching for yourself
in all the wrong men
who have taken you
for themselves
and then discarded you
once they were finished.

Raise your vibration
and let this last heartbreak
be the final one.
You are made of pure light
and nobody can take
away the love you have
for yourself.

Promise yourself to be
so strong that the next man
who comes into your life
knows there is
an entire universe
inside of you
that deserves respect.

# Hope

How do you continue to thrive
in a hurting world when you offer
your vulnerable gift and it is
completely rejected?

I am longing for the day when I am
in the sunshine once again, arms wide
open, yellow hair in the wind,
a wide smile across my face.

I am longing for this peace to take
hold of my ache so I can breathe again.
Some days are divine, and some days
I am drowning, clawing my way out.

Remember it is okay to not be okay.
One day I will be in this stillness
with a heart wide open ready
to love again, and it will be cherished.

# Om Shanti

Be brave, strong woman.

You already have everything
you need within you
to have the life
you keep wanting.

# One Day at a Time

Allow your healing
to take as long as it needs.

You will know you've
arrived home

when you feel free
in your breath.

# Love Will Change the World

I will choose love
because it is the steadfast
existence I see when
I look into the eyes of all beings.

It is an easy task to hate
but even on the days
I feel hopeless or betrayed
I choose to practice love

to hold my own heart
gentle with both hands
when the night turns
moonless, because love
takes bravery,
strength, courage.

# Patience

Slow down,
breathe deep,
nourish your cells

because after all
the greatest relationship
you will ever have

is with yourself.

# Thank You

The first time you let me stay the night
we listened to shooting stars fall
across the black night sky. You knew
I needed someone to lie my body next to.

It was numb outside as the town
was covered in knee deep snow.
You gave me a safe home
when I felt the most alone.

The way we used to love each other
was human, as I slept next to you
in the early morning and felt your
warm touch reach for mine.

You gave me a safe home
in your heart that dreadful season.
I'll never forget you or the winter
where we healed together.

# Awakening

Maybe we experience loss
because the universe
is making room for something
better in our life.

After all, you deserve a love
who will hold you when you shake
rather than curse you alone.

Never forget your worth,
even when the loss of him
soaks your bed with tears.

This is your awakening
to the life you have always
dreamt of; don't let days
pass you by
because he couldn't
love you.

# Her Eyes

As I grieve and watch water drip
into the soil beneath me
I miraculously witness the earth
grow her flowers.
Little green seedlings
pierce through solid ground
breathing in golden sun,
drinking in lachrymal tears
and they are showing me
life is ripening within.
I can almost hear them
murmur the words
"Never give up."

# Courageous

No longer do I need a man
to complete me, because when
I love myself,
my worth, my earthy magic,
I know I deserve someone
who never makes me question
these scars on my heart.

# You Are Healing

Be gentle, be gentle
Be gentle with yourself.

I love you. I am listening.

# The Poets Garden

There is a light that begins to linger
      in spring, and I ponder on how
            Asiatic lilies emerge through thick,
                crystalized dirt.

Some are plum colored and burgundy,
      it reminds me of my childhood home
            as a little girl peeking behind enormous
                sunflower faces, cadmium yellow.

What an amazing creation
      to witness when
            the season evolves before
                my eyes wake at dawn.

Suddenly, I am immersed in honor,
      kindness, virtue, freedom
            colorful and sweet,
                bowing to this assortment of beauty.

The earth is a gift
      we must always cherish
            while we still can.

# Lover of Alaska

In winter, I wake to pitch darkness
and gradually watch the sun peek its rays
over the horizon as it sits until three hours
after it's risen. I lace up my boots,
pull on my puffy jacket, and prepare to conquer
the icy snow fall, thick scarf over rosy nose.
Chopping wood, starting fire, burning flames.

In summer, I wake to manic solstice hours
where the midnight sun shines
and the lush earth grows evergreens, hemlocks,
gardens, squash, and the canopy rains fall
down to my braided hair and bare feet.
The majestic whales break through the surface
expelling breath through their blowhole.
I can see them dancing from my kitchen window.

The wanton stars are singing a song
to nourish the earth in the universe
and I cannot help but feel
the momentous music in my bones.
Everything is alive, waking up, and
rising in this warm luminescence
as morning breaks through darkness.

I am not afraid to feel everything.
Why are we hiding beneath sheets when
we should be singing along with creatures
and celestial bodies who survive harsh winters?
When people ask why I live in Alaska,
it is because it teaches me to be a stronger woman.
I am rising no matter the elements.

# Nevertheless, She Survived

I want to share with you
how the practice of yoga
and meditation saved my life.

At first, it was subtle,
as though the practice knew
how to slip beneath the surface,
into the core of my existence
without my even realizing.

I went into the class during
the darkest winter of my life.
I remember it clearly. It was early
December, I barely made it in time.
I was searching for something,
anything to occupy my mind.

My heart was bruised, shattered, defeated.
I studied yoga before, but during
this specific season
its secret came to save me.

Savasana, corpse pose, the last pose
before you wake for the second time
in the day and give gratitude for showing
up. I lay in this relaxed position,
and for the first time I felt whole.

Energy inside of my body rose
as a brilliant, golden light,
up my spine into the space of the chest
and throat, filling me with peace.

In this moment, my life changed.
I was already safe and whole.
No longer would I reach for something
so far away when it was there all along.

Stillness is magic. It truly is.
If you want to raise your vibration,
sit with yourself.
There is no wrong way to listen
to your own heart beating.
Watch thoughts
float in, and float out.

You have a story to share.
Listen to it. Believe it.

# Alive

I'm sitting in a cafe drinking a hot americano
and I'm watching the rain slide down the side
of the window, elated.
Two days ago, I almost ended my life
but this afternoon I woke up
to see what happens if I keep thriving.
There is nothing more powerful
than choosing life after you have
been hurt. This is where magic
is made and transformation resides
because in the moment right before
you give up, suddenly something
shifts and the whole universe
works in your favor if you choose
to open your eyes and see the beauty
all around you. This beauty is not
screaming for attention. It is subtle
and magnificent like the dog sleeping
next to the fireplace on a crisp morning,
a child's awe in a floating bubble, or
my grandmothers smile when she sees me again.

Instead of giving up
I choose to breathe in all of life's elements
in every possible way before my last breath.

I am alive.
I am alive.
I am alive.

# The Collective

The cold, starlit sea before me
shimmered in unwavering delight.
She was speaking with her mouth wide open
as I stretched my hands into the arctic frost.

I remember the shivering, shrinking, vanishing
of darkness and listened to her whisper my story,
how I have many more days to be whole
in this sway of life between the sun and moon.

Speaking consciousness is a language
I am forever grateful to receive
as the birds open their eyes and take
their first morning breath to greet me.

# Gardening

I am planting seeds
in the garden of hope.

Its soiled texture is smooth
and soft like a sweet berry.

I am beginning to notice
the decadent flowers flourish

As the earth beats
"I'm not finished with you yet."

# Om Namah Shivaya

I hear my beating heart
and I know I belong
to something bigger
than myself.

The forest trees are waking to the wind
and I can feel it blow into my long, flaxen hair.
Autumn is coming again, as she always does,
but this time, I am ready.

# About the Author

Kara Troglin is a yoga teacher and writer originally from Fort Worth, Texas. She received her B.A. in creative writing from the University of Arkansas, where she also spent time studying plant biology. She is a lover of nature and traveling the world. Her biggest passion in life is sharing healing and compassion with all of humanity through yoga, writing, and genuine smiles. She currently resides in her favorite seaside town, Seward, Alaska.

CPSIA information can be obtained
at www.ICGtesting.com
Printed in the USA
FSHW012050160219
55729FS